Hot Math Topics

Problem Solving, Communication, and Reasoning

Algebraic Reasoning

Grade 5

Carole Greenes
Linda Schulman Dacey
Rika Spungin

Dale Seymour Publications®
Parsippany, New Jersey

Acknowledgment: The authors wish to acknowledge the outstanding contributions of Mali Apple in the production of the *Hot Math Topics* series. She has given careful attention to the content, design, and art, and helped shepherd the program through from its inception to its completion. Thank you, Mali.

Dale Seymour Publications

An imprint of Pearson Learning
299 Jefferson Road
Parsippany, New Jersey 07054-0480
www.pearsonlearning.com
1-800-321-3106

Editorial Manager: Carolyn Coyle
Project Editor: Mali Apple
Production/Manufacturing Director: Janet Yearian
Production/Manufacturing Manager: Karen Edmonds
Production/Manufacturing Coordinator: Lorraine Allen
Art Director: Jim O'Shea
Cover Design: Tracey Munz
Cover and Interior Illustrations: Jared Lee
Computer Graphics: Alan Noyes

ISBN 0-7690-0839-9

1 2 3 4 5 6 7 8 9 10-ML-04 03 02 01 00

This Book Is Printed
On Recycled Paper

Contents

Introduction

Why Was *Hot Math Topics* Developed?

The *Hot Math Topics* series was developed for several reasons:

- to offer students practice and maintenance of previously learned skills and concepts
- to enhance problem solving and mathematical reasoning abilities
- to build literacy skills
- to nurture collaborative learning behaviors

Practicing and maintaining concepts and skills

Although textbooks and core curriculum materials do treat the topics explored in this series, their treatment is often limited by the lesson format and the page size. As a consequence, there are often not enough opportunities for students to practice newly acquired concepts and skills related to the topics, or to connect the topics to other content areas. *Hot Math Topics* provides the necessary practice and mathematical connections.

Similarly, core instructional programs often do not do a very good job of helping students maintain their skills. Although textbooks do include reviews of previously learned material, they are frequently limited to sidebars or boxed-off areas on one or two pages in each chapter, with four or five exercises in each box. Each set of problems is intended only as a sampling of previously taught topics, rather than as a complete review. In the selection and placement of the review exercises, little or no attention is given to levels of complexity of the problems. By contrast, *Hot Math Topics* targets specific topics and gives students more experience with concepts and skills related to them. The problems are sequenced by difficulty, allowing students to hone their skills. And, because they are not tied to specific lessons, the problems can be used at any time.

Enhancing problem solving and mathematical reasoning abilities

Hot Math Topics presents students with situations in which they may use a variety of problem solving strategies, including

- designing and conducting experiments to generate or collect data
- guessing, checking, and revising guesses
- organizing data in lists or tables in order to identify patterns and relationships
- choosing appropriate computational algorithms and deciding on a sequence of computations
- using inverse operations in "work backward" solution paths

For their solutions, students are also required to bring to bear various methods of reasoning, including

- deductive reasoning
- inductive reasoning
- proportional reasoning

For example, to solve clue-type problems, students must reason deductively and make inferences about mathematical relationships in order to generate candidates for the solutions and to hone in on those that meet all of the problem's conditions.

To identify and continue a pattern and then write a rule for finding the next term in that pattern, students must reason inductively.

To compute unit prices and work with ratios, students must reason proportionally.

To compare magnitudes of numbers and identify relationships among numbers, students must apply their number sense skills.

Building communication and literacy skills

Hot Math Topics offers students opportunities to write and talk about mathematical ideas. For many problems, students must describe their solution paths, justify their solutions, give their opinions, or write or tell stories.

Some problems have multiple solution methods. With these problems, students may have to compare their methods with those of their peers and talk about how their approaches are alike and different.

Other problems have multiple solutions, requiring students to confer to be sure they have found all possible answers.

Nurturing collaborative learning behaviors

Several of the problems can be solved by students working together. Some are designed specifically as partner problems. By working collaboratively, students can develop expertise in posing questions that call for clarification or verification, brainstorming solution strategies, and following another person's line of reasoning.

What Is in *Algebraic Reasoning?*

This book contains 100 problems and tasks that focus on algebraic reasoning. The mathematics content, the mathematical connections, the problem solving strategies, and the communication skills that are emphasized are described below.

Mathematics content

These problems and tasks require students to

- understand equality
- replace variables with numbers to solve equations and inequalities
- identify, describe, continue, and generalize patterns
- identify and describe relations
- use variables to write equations to represent relationships
- describe function rules using words and symbols
- use deductive, inductive, and proportional reasoning to solve problems
- use substitution to solve algebraic problems
- identify relationships in graphs and Venn diagrams
- identify and construct different representations of the same algebraic relationship

Mathematical connections

In these problems and tasks, connections are made to these other topic areas:

- arithmetic
- geometry
- graphs
- measurement
- number theory
- statistics

Problem solving strategies

Algebraic Reasoning problems and tasks offer students opportunities to use one or more of several problem solving strategies.

- **Formulate Questions:** When data are presented in displays or text form, students must pose one or more questions that can be answered using the given data.

- **Complete Stories:** When confronted with an incomplete story, students must supply the missing information and then check that the story makes sense.

- **Organize Information:** To ensure that all possible solution candidates for a problem are considered, students may have to organize information by drawing a picture, making a list, or constructing an equation

- **Guess, Check, and Revise:** In some problems, students have to identify candidates for the solution and then check whether those candidates match the conditions of the problem. If the conditions are not satisfied, other possible solutions must be generated and verified.

- **Identify and Continue Patterns:** To identify the next term or terms in a sequence, students have to recognize the relationship between successive terms and then generalize that relationship.

- **Use Logic:** Students have to reason deductively, from clues, to make inferences about the solution to a problem. They must reason proportionally to determine which of two buys is better. They have to reason inductively to continue numeric and shape patterns.

- **Work Backward:** In some problems, the output is given and students must determine the input by identifying mathematical relationships between the input and output and applying inverse operations.

Communication skills

Problems and tasks in *Algebraic Reasoning* are designed to stimulate communication. As part of the solution process, students may have to

- describe their thinking steps
- describe patterns and rules
- find alternate solution methods and solution paths
- formulate problems for classmates to solve
- compare answers and solution methods with classmates
- describe mathematical relationships presented in graphs, in tables, and with symbols

These communication skills are enhanced when students interact with one another and with the teacher. By communicating both orally and in writing, students develop their understanding and use of the language of mathematics.

How Can *Hot Math Topics* Be Used?

The problems may be used as practice of newly learned concepts and skills, as maintenance of previously learned ideas, and as enrichment experiences for early finishers or more advanced students.

They may be used in class or assigned for homework. If used during class, they may be selected to complement lessons dealing with a specific topic or assigned every week as a means of keeping skills alive and well. Because the problems often require the application of various problem solving strategies and reasoning methods, they may also form the basis of whole-class lessons whose goals are to develop expertise with specific problem solving strategies or methods.

The problems, which are sequenced from least to most difficult, may be used by students working in pairs or on their own. The selection of problems may be made by the teacher or the students based on their needs or interests. If the plan is for students to choose problems, you may wish to copy individual problems onto card stock and laminate them, and establish a problem card file.

To facilitate record keeping, a Management Chart is provided on page 6. The chart can be duplicated so that there is one for each student. As a problem is completed, the space corresponding to that problem's number may be shaded. An Award Certificate is included on page 6 as well.

How Can Student Performance Be Assessed?

Algebraic Reasoning problems and tasks provide you with opportunities to assess students'

- algebraic reasoning
- logical reasoning methods
- computation abilities
- problem solving abilities
- communication skills

Observations

Keeping anecdotal records helps you to remember important information you gain as you observe students at work. To make observations more manageable, limit each observation to a group of from four to six students or to one of the areas noted above. You may find that using index cards facilitates the recording process.

Discussions

Many of the *Algebraic Reasoning* problems and tasks allow for multiple answers or may be solved in a variety of ways. This built-in richness motivates students to discuss their work with one another. Small groups or class discussions are appropriate. As students share their approaches to the problems, you will gain additional insights into their content knowledge, mathematical reasoning, and communication abilities.

Scoring responses

You may wish to holistically score students' responses to the problems and tasks. The simple scoring rubric below uses three levels: high, medium, and low.

Portfolios

Having students store their responses to the problems in *Hot Math Topics* portfolios allows them to see improvement in their work over time. You may want to have them

High	Medium	Low
• Solution demonstrates that the student knows the concepts and skills.	• Solution demonstrates that the student has some knowledge of the concepts and skills.	• Solution shows that the student has little or no grasp of the concepts and skills.
• Solution is complete and thorough.	• Solution is complete.	• Solution is incomplete or contains major errors.
• Student communicates effectively.	• Student communicates somewhat clearly.	• Student does not communicate effectively.

choose examples of their best responses for inclusion in their permanent portfolios, accompanied by explanations as to why each was chosen.

Students and the assessment process

Involving students in the assessment process is central to the development of their abilities to reflect on their own work, to understand the assessment standards to which they are held accountable, and to take ownership for their own learning. Young children may find the reflective process difficult, but with your coaching, they can develop such skills.

Discussion may be needed to help students better understand your standards for performance. Ask students such questions as, "What does it mean to communicate *clearly*?" "What is a *complete* response?" Some students may want to use the high-medium-low rubric to score their responses.

Participation in peer-assessment tasks will also help students to better understand the performance standards. In pairs or small groups, students can review each other's responses and offer feedback. Opportunities to revise work may then be given.

What Additional Materials Are Needed?

Although the use of calculators is not required, students may find them beneficial for some problems. No other materials are necessary.

Management Chart

Name _____

When a problem or task is completed, shade the box with that number.

1	2	3	4	5	6	7	8	9	10
11	12	13	14	15	16	17	18	19	20
21	22	23	24	25	26	27	28	29	30
31	32	33	34	35	36	37	38	39	40
41	42	43	44	45	46	47	48	49	50
51	52	53	54	55	56	57	58	59	60
61	62	63	64	65	66	67	68	69	70
71	72	73	74	75	76	77	78	79	80
81	82	83	84	85	86	87	88	89	90
91	92	93	94	95	96	97	98	99	100

© Dale Seymour Publications®

Award Certificate

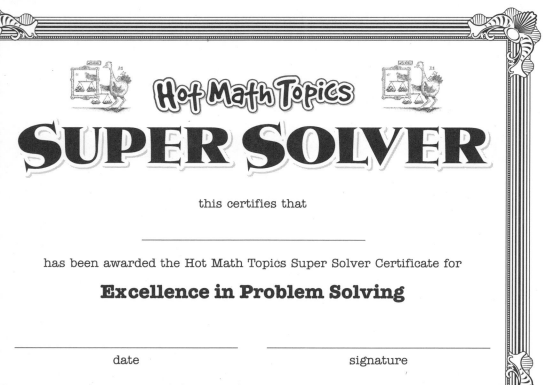

Hot Math Topics

SUPER SOLVER

this certifies that

_____

has been awarded the Hot Math Topics Super Solver Certificate for

Excellence in Problem Solving

_____ _____
date   signature

© Dale Seymour Publications®

Problems
and Tasks

Order the boys by height.

Start with the tallest.

- Jed is shorter than Jeff.
- Jeff is taller than Jin Lee, but shorter than Jared.
- Jonas is taller than Jared.
- Jed is not the shortest.

1

The pattern in the array of numbers continues.

Counting from left to right, what is the 90th number in row 85?

How did you figure it out?

2

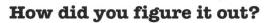

Row 1 ... 1

Row 2 ... 1 2 1

Row 3 ... 1 2 3 2 1

Row 4 ... 1 2 3 4 3 2 1

Row 5 ... 1 2 3 4 5 4 3 2 1

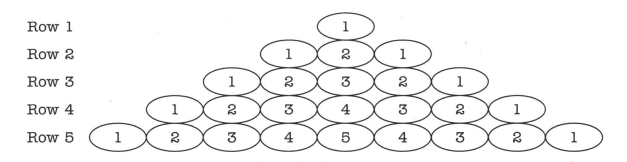

Write 2 more questions about this array of numbers.

Give them to a classmate to solve.

Look at the table.

Describe a rule for getting each output from the input.

Input	Output
1	2
2	5
3	8
4	11
5	14

What's the rule?

Make up your own input-output rule.

List 5 input-output pairs.

Have a classmate identify your rule.

I've been working out.

- On the first day, I did 1 sit-up.
- One the second day, I did 2 sit-ups.
- On the third day, I did 4 sit-ups.
- On the fourth day, I did 7 sit-ups.
- On the fifth day, I did 11 sit-ups.

If I continue this pattern, how many sit-ups will I do on the tenth day?

3, 4, 5, 6...

$$A > B$$
$$B > C$$
$$C > D$$
$$D > A$$

Can the statements on the banner be true?

Explain why or why not.

- -

The scales give clues about how the weights of the objects are related.

Make up weights for the 3 objects that make sense.

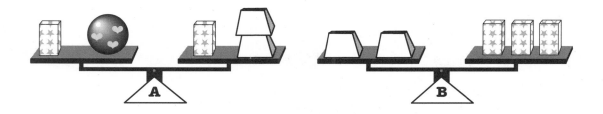

 = ____ pounds   = ____ pounds   = ____ pounds

Is another answer possible?

Explain.

January is month 1.
February is month 2.
•
•
•
December is month 12.

What is the day and the month of my birthday?

- The sum of the day and the month is 22.
- The difference of the day and month is 8.

My birthday is _____.

- -

Mr. Maretti's bank charges $1.50 a month for his checking account.

The bank also charges 20¢ for each check he writes.

Mr. Maretti does not want to be charged more than $4.00 a month.

What is the greatest number of checks he can write in a month?

List the steps you used to answer the question.

The sum of 3 whole numbers is 16.

Two of the numbers add to the third number.

What could the 3 numbers be?

Make a list.

What is the start number?

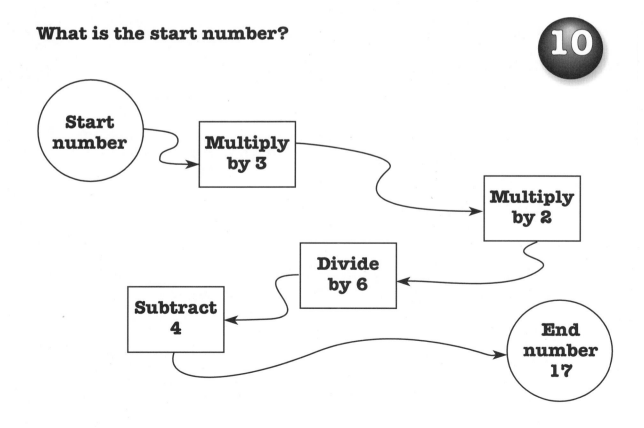

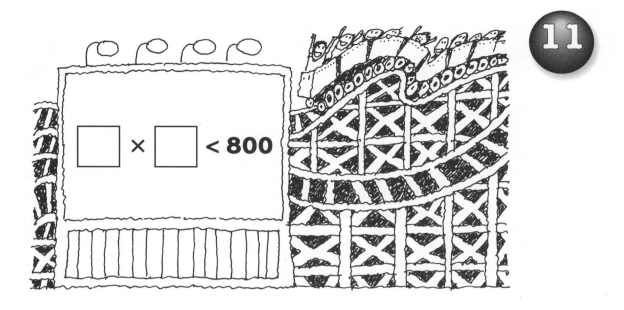

11

$$\boxed{} \times \boxed{} < 800$$

What is the greatest whole number that makes the statement on the sign true?

- -

12

One 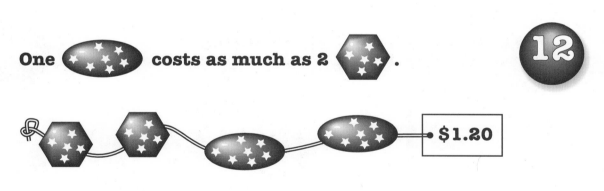 costs as much as 2 ⬡ .

$1.20

Work with a classmate.

Tell 2 ways to find the cost of the bead chain below.

?

13

8 SQUIGGLES = 2 WIGGLES

1 WIGGLE = 4 JIGGLES

What is the relationship of squiggles to jiggles?

- -

The graph shows Jim's speed during part of his bicycle ride.

Tell a story about this part of his ride.

14

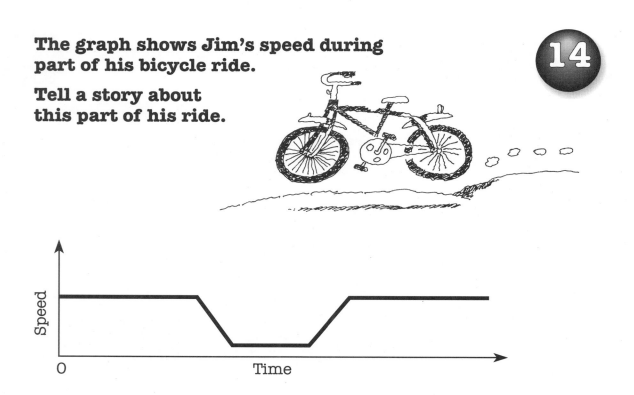

Speed

0   Time

There are 30 rows in section A of the stadium.

Below are the first 5 rows.

Row 5	25	26	27	28	29	30	31	32	33	34	35
Row 4		16	17	18	19	20	21	22	23	24	
Row 3			9	10	11	12	13	14	15		
Row 2				4	5	6	7	8			
Row 1					1	2	3				

Section A

How many seats are in row 30?

How many seats are in section A?

Explain how you decided.

- -

How many vowels are in the first 800 letters of this pattern?

MOONGLOWMOONGLOWMOONGLOW...

20 is the first common multiple of 4 and 5.

What is the 12th common multiple of 4 and 5?

- -

There are 24 guppies, 3 goldfish, and 3 angelfish in the fish tank.

This means there are 8 guppies for every goldfish and every angelfish.

Some of the guppies are sold.

Now there are 5 guppies for every goldfish and for every angelfish.

How many guppies were sold?

Add across. Add down.

The same shapes are the same number.

The numbers in the circles are the row and column sums.

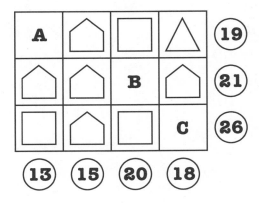

A = _____   B = _____   C = _____

- -

What is the fewest number of marbles Noah and Regina could have?

Noah could have _____ marbles and Regina could have _____ marbles.

Tell how you know.

If Regina has 6 marbles, how many marbles does Noah have?

If you know that Noah has **N** marbles, write a rule to tell the number Regina has: _____

What is the side length of Rosa's square?

The number of inches in the perimeter of my square is the same as the number of square inches in its area.

- -

Let *n* stand for each of the numbers 1 to 10.

Write each number in the correct section of the Venn diagram: A, B, C, or D.

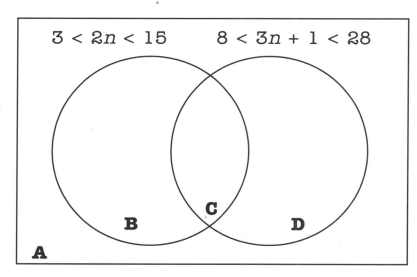

$$3 < 2n < 15 \qquad 8 < 3n + 1 < 28$$

A   B   C   D

Venn Diagram

1   2
3   4
5   6
7   8
9   10

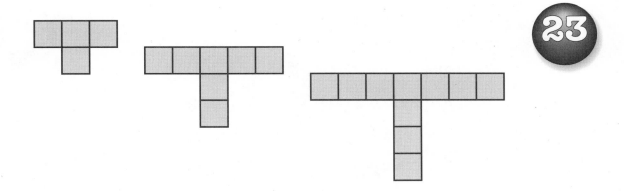

The pattern of T-shapes continues.

How many squares are in the T-shape that has 8 squares below the horizontal row of squares?

How did you decide?

- -

↑ means add 9	↓ means subtract 9
→ means add 1	← means subtract 1
↗ means add 10	↙ means subtract 10
↖ means add 8	↘ means subtract 8

Write arrows in the box to go from 4 to 81.

Use the least number of arrows possible.

4	81

$$k \times k \times k = 729$$

What is the value of $k + k$?

- -

Match the "if" and "then" statements to make true sentences.

1. If $n = 4$,

a. then $5n = 81$.

2. If $n = 210$,

b. then $(n + 3) \times 7 = 49$.

3. If $n = 16.20$,

c. then $n \div 70 = 3$.

4. If $n = 1$,

d. then $n \times n = 1$.

I bought a pineapple and 12 bananas for $8.00.

The pineapple cost as much as 8 bananas.

How much did 1 banana cost?

- -

Circle 34.

Find 2 numbers on the chart that have a mean of 34.

Find 3 more pairs of numbers that have a mean of 34.

1	2	3	4	5	6	7	8	9	10
11	12	13	14	15	16	17	18	19	20
21	22	23	24	25	26	27	28	29	30
31	32	33	34	35	36	37	38	39	40
41	42	43	44	45	46	47	48	49	50
51	52	53	54	55	56	57	58	59	60
61	62	63	64	65	66	67	68	69	70
71						77	78	79	80

Compare your pairs of numbers with a classmate.

What do you notice?

What is operation **doing?**

Describe the rule in words.

6  4 = 16   3  5 = 11

0  9 = 9   9  0 = 18

Fill in the squares.

2  1 = ☐   7  3 = ☐

☐  4 = 12   8  ☐ = 20

Jenna, Tess, and Reva have side-by-side lockers, numbered consecutively from left to right.

Jenna's locker is the farthest to the left.

Tess's locker is in the middle.

Let △ represent Jenna's locker number.

How would you write

- Tess's locker number?
- Reva's locker number?

The sum of their locker numbers is 399.

What is the number on Tess's locker?

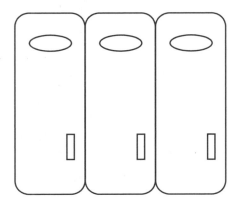

The **Ring-a-Ding** phone company charges $2.00 a month plus 6¢ a minute for long-distance calls.

The **R.U. There?** company charges 10¢ a minute for long-distance calls, with no additional monthly charge.

Minutes	Charge	
	Ring-a-Ding	R.U. There?
0	$2.00	$0.00
5	2.30	0.50
10	2.60	1.00

Ms. Canton averages 1 hour of long-distance calls each month.

Which phone company should she use?

How did you decide?

- -

$$1 + 3 = 4$$
$$1 + 3 + 5 = 9$$
$$1 + 3 + 5 + 7 = 16$$
$$1 + 3 + 5 + 7 + 9 = 25$$
$$1 + 3 + 5 + 7 + 9 + 11 = 36$$

The first _2_ odd numbers add to 4.

The first _3_ odd numbers add to 9.

The first _4_ odd numbers add to 16.

The first ___ odd numbers add to 400.

Look at the example.

Follow the steps for 3 more numbers using columns 1, 2, and 3.

What do you notice?

Steps	Example	(1)	(2)	(3)	(4)
				Columns	
Think of a number.	15	____	____	____	▲
Multiply it by 2.	30	____	____	____	____
Add 10.	40	____	____	____	____
Multiply by 5.	200	____	____	____	____
Subtract 50.	150	____	____	____	____

Suppose the number is the secret number ▲.

Fill in the blanks under column 4.

- -

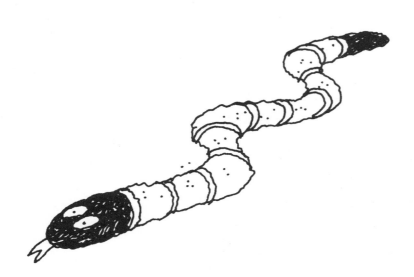

The snake ate 80 legs.

He ate 3 more spiders than ants.

How many spiders did he eat?

How many ants did he eat?

The graph represents Geoff's, Jerome's, and Kiran's bike speeds during a 20-mile race.

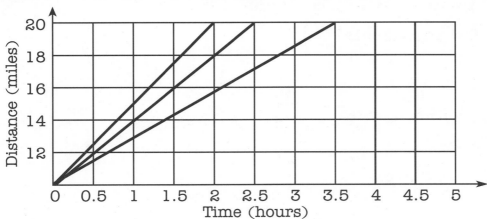

The race started at 8:30 A.M.

Geoff won. Jerome came in last.

At what time did Jerome finish the race?

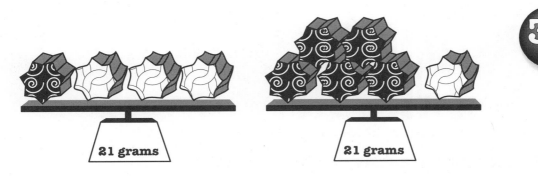

Each  is the same number of grams.

Each ✦ is the same number of grams.

How many grams is the ✿ ?

How many grams is the ✦ ?

Describe your thinking steps.

Suppose you count by 3s from 3 to 999.

How many even numbers would you say?

How did you decide?

- -

$$(\text{✦} \times 10) \div \text{☀} = 4$$

Fill in the table.

Find 5 pairs of whole numbers for ✦ and ☀

that make the equation above true.

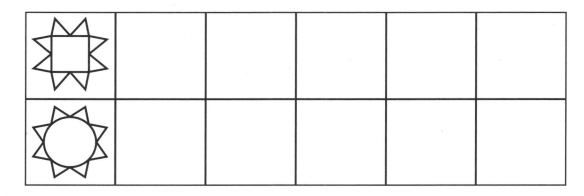

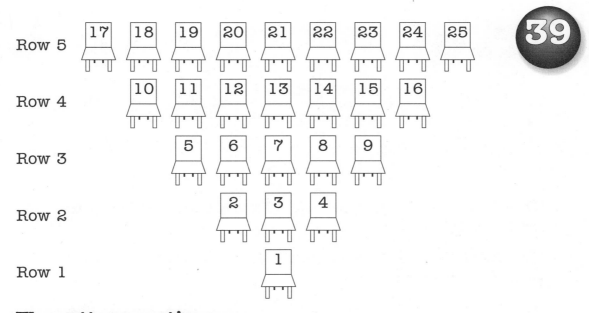

Row 5 17 18 19 20 21 22 23 24 25

Row 4 10 11 12 13 14 15 16

Row 3 5 6 7 8 9

Row 2 2 3 4

Row 1 1

The pattern continues.

I'm sitting in seat 423. Which row am I in?

Tell how you decided.

39

The volume of the cube is 125 cubic inches.

What is its surface area?

40

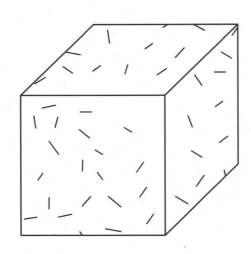

The Swim Club charges a $50 membership fee plus $40 per month.

The Cool Pool Club charges a $175 membership fee plus $20 per month.

After how many months is the total charge for the Cool Pool Club less than the total charge for the Swim Club?

- -

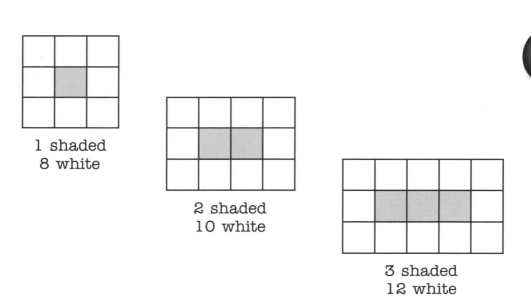

1 shaded
8 white

2 shaded
10 white

3 shaded
12 white

How many white squares will be in the figure with 100 shaded squares?

Explain how you know.

© Dale Seymour Publications®

$906 \div n = m$

If *n* is 6, what is the value of *m*?

If the value of *n* increases, how will the value of *m* change?

If the value of *n* decreases, what happens to the value of *m*?

- -

The same shapes are the same numbers.

$\square \times \square = \mathbf{49}$

$\square \times \triangle = \mathbf{56}$

$\triangle + \pentagon = \mathbf{18}$

$\square \times \triangle \times \pentagon = \mathbf{?}$

45

Two-hundred eighty more than some number is half of 750.

What is the number?

- -

Maria and Leo both worked all summer.

46

We earned a total of $1250.

You earned $250 more than I did.

MARIA

LEO

How much money did Maria earn?

How much money did Leo earn?

The scales are balanced.

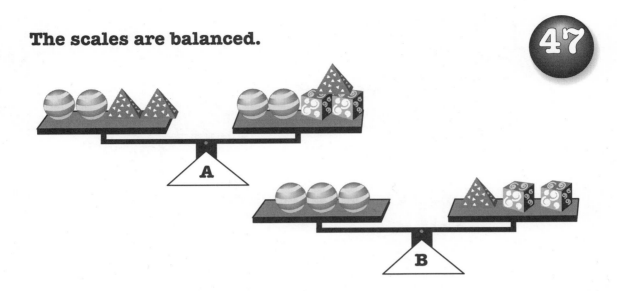

Order the 3 objects—pyramid, sphere, and cube—from heaviest to lightest.

How did you decide on the order?

- -

Joe, Sy, and Ed are each thinking of a decimal number.

Joe's number is _____ .

Sy's number is _____ .

Ed's number is _____ .

Here are 2 collections of toys for sale.

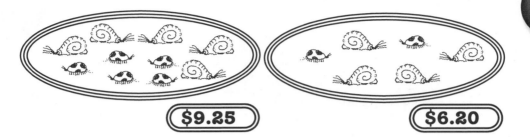

$9.25 $6.20

Fill in the prices for the toy collections below.

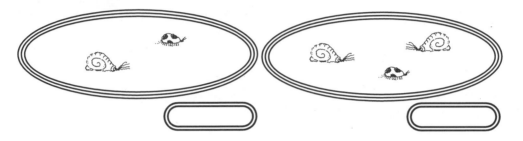

One 🐌 costs _____. One 🐌 costs _____.

- -

Make a copy of this month's calendar. Choose a number that falls on a weekday. Draw an H with your number in the middle. Find the sum of the 7 numbers in the H.

Do this for other H's. Keep a record of your results.

What is the middle number if the sum is 161? How did you decide?

S	M	T	W	T	F	S
				1	2	3
4	5	6	7	8	9	10
11	12	13	14	15	16	17
18	19	20	21	22	23	24
25	26	27	28	29	30	31

This is a 14-H.

Middle Number	Sum
14	98

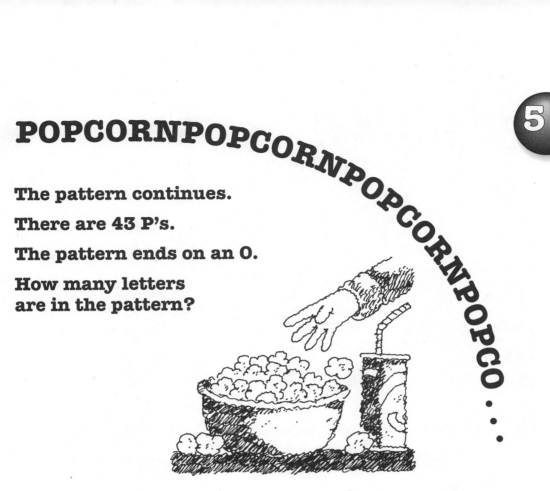

POPCORNPOPCORNPOPCORNPOPCO...

The pattern continues.

There are 43 P's.

The pattern ends on an O.

How many letters
are in the pattern?

How do you get the output from the input?

Write the rule.

Input	Output
0	−1
1	5
2	11
3	17
4	23
5	29

10% of what number is equal to 20% of 400?

- -

The pattern continues.

How many small white squares are in square 28?

How do you know?

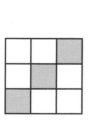
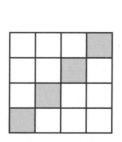
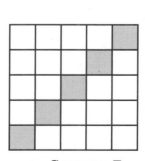
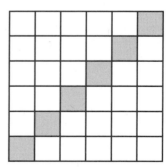

Square 1   Square 2   Square 3   Square 4

Start with the 5 in the square.

Fill the circle with an operation and a number so that when you follow all the arrows, you end on 5.

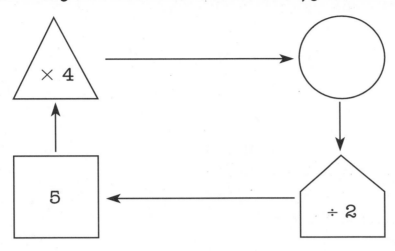

Can you find another way to fill the circle?

Write about how you decided.

- -

This graph could show the relationship between the number of hours Leila baby-sat and the amount of money she earned.

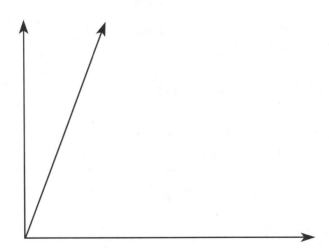

Describe another relationship this graph could show.

Describe a relationship this graph does not show.

The numbers in the circles are added in pairs.

The sum of each pair is on the line joining them.

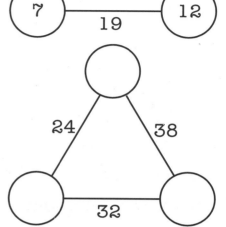

In the second triangle, only the sum of each pair of numbers is given.

Write the missing numbers in the circles.

Tell how you decided.

- -

Marcelo bought 3 pens and 2 pencils for $5.25.

Lana bought 1 pen and 2 pencils for $2.75.

All the pens cost the same amount.

All the pencils cost the same amount.

What is the total cost of 1 pen and 1 pencil?

How did you solve this problem?

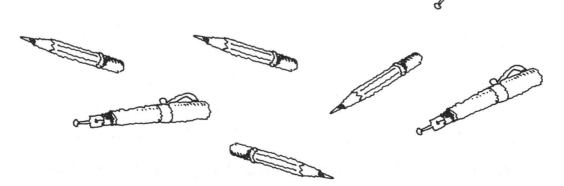

There are nickels in the 3 bags.

The numbers tell how many nickels are in each pair of bags.

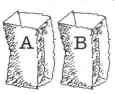 

22   18   20

What is the value of the nickels

in bag A? _____   in bag B? _____   in bag C? _____

Describe your thinking steps.

- -

The letter *w* stands for a whole number.

What values for *w* make this statement true?

$17 < 2w + 5 < 48$

Camp Runaround is a summer baseball camp.

The ratio of coaches to campers at Camp Runaround is 2:9.

The total number of coaches and campers is 440.

How many campers are there?

Which is the better buy?

Sale!
3 videos for $20!

Sale!
4 videos for $25!

Describe 2 ways to decide.

© Dale Seymour Publications®

Pedro, Jeff, and Darry collect sports cards.

- Let p represent the number of cards in Pedro's collection.

- Let $p - 3$ represent the number of cards in Jeff's collection.

- Let $p + 3$ represent the number of cards in Darry's collection.

Altogether, the 3 friends have 189 sports cards.

How many does Pedro have?

How did you decide?

A skateboard and a helmet cost $120.

The helmet costs $88 less than the skateboard.

What is the cost of 6 helmets and 2 skateboards?

65

Find the values of the letters.

$m =$ _____

$n =$ _____

- -

66

Ozzie's Pizza Shop

2 cheese pizzas 3 cheese pizzas
1 bottle of water 3 bottles of water
$22.50 $37.50

What is the price of a bottle of water?

Imagine that you leave your seat and walk to the pencil sharpener.

You sharpen your pencil and return to your seat.

Which graph might show your distance from your seat during this time?

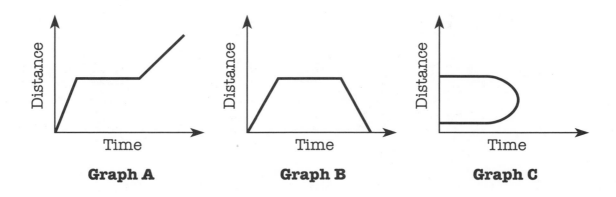

Graph A   **Graph B**   **Graph C**

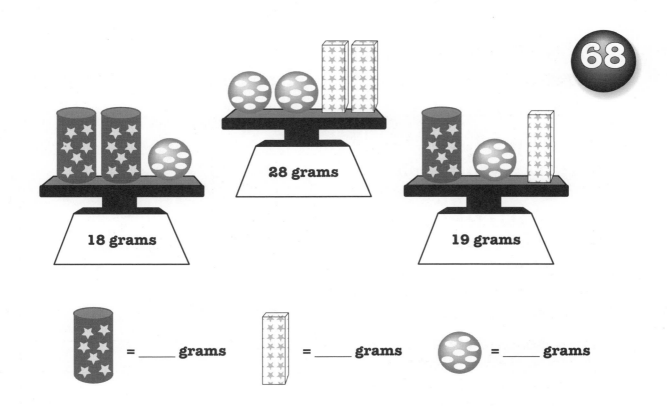

List the steps you used to find each mass.

The pattern continues. In which row and column is the number 60? Tell how you know.

	Column A	Column B	Column C	Column D	Column E	Column F
Row 1	1	2	3	4	5	6
Row 2	12	11	10	9	8	7
Row 3	13	14	15	16	17	18
Row 4	24	23	22	21	20	19

Make up another question about a number in the chart greater than 100. Give your question to a classmate to answer.

- -

Choose 3 consecutive numbers.

- Let *a*, *b*, and *c* represent your numbers.

- Multiply *a* and *c*.

- Multiply *b* by itself.

- Record your results in a table.

Repeat this for 4 more sets of consecutive numbers.

Describe the pattern you see in words.

Now describe the pattern using *a* for the first number, *b* for the second number, and *c* for the third number.

First number a	Second number b	Third number c	$a \times c$	$b \times b$
3	4	5	15	16

Use the numbers on the sign to fill in the story.

The story must make sense.

Miki has $_____ in quarters, dimes, and nickels.

The ratio of the number of quarters to the number of dimes is _____ to _____.

Miki has _____ quarters and _____ dimes.

She also has _____ nickels.

Ossy Trich does home repairs.

I charge $50 to make a house call.

I charge $40 for each hour of work.

Let *h* represent the hours she worked, and let *C* represent the total charge.

Write an equation to represent Ms. Trich's total charge when the number of hours she worked is known.

Use the equation to find Ms. Trich's charge for 7.5 hours of work at your home.

What is the 🍌 **doing?**

0 🍌 3 = 3   10 🍌 3 = 33   100 🍌 3 = 303

7 🍌 4 = 25   50 🍌 20 = 170   103 🍌 500 = 809

Use the 🍌 **rule to solve these problems.**

64 🍌 110 = _____

_____ 🍌 20 = 290

93 🍌 _____ = 312

- -

2 STARS = 3 STARBURSTS

6 STARBURSTS = 5 SUNSTARS

15 SUNSTARS = 9 BURSTING SUNSTARS

18 bursting sunstars = _____ stars

A $5 bill is about 6 inches long.

Suppose lots of $5 bills are laid end-to-end to make a line 1 mile long. What will be the total value of the line of bills?

- -

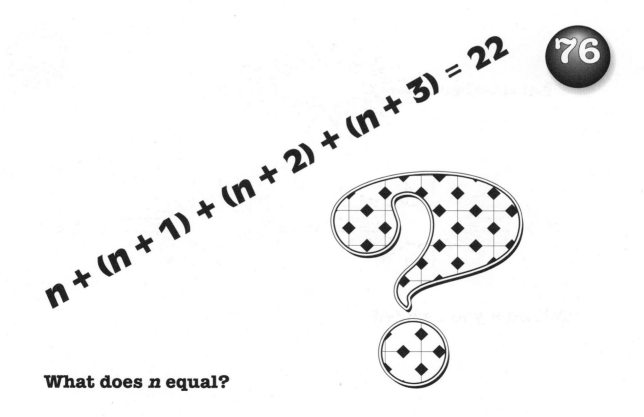

$n + (n + 1) + (n + 2) + (n + 3) = 22$

What does *n* equal?

I'm thinking of a number less than 500.

It is divisible by 2, 3, and 5.

Its digits add to 12.

What is the number?

Is another answer possible?

- -

What number is 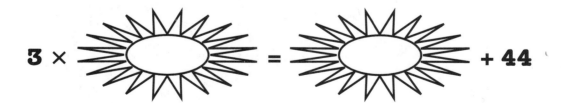 ?

$$3 \times \bigcirc = \bigcirc + 44$$

Tell how you decided.

(79)

 = _____ kg

 = _____ kg

 = _____ kg

 = _____ kg

- -

The pattern of building continues.

(80)

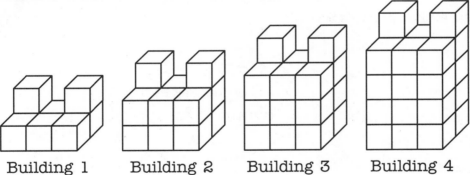

Building 1   Building 2   Building 3   Building 4

How many ⬜ are needed to make building 50?

How can you use the building number to find the number of ⬜ in the building?

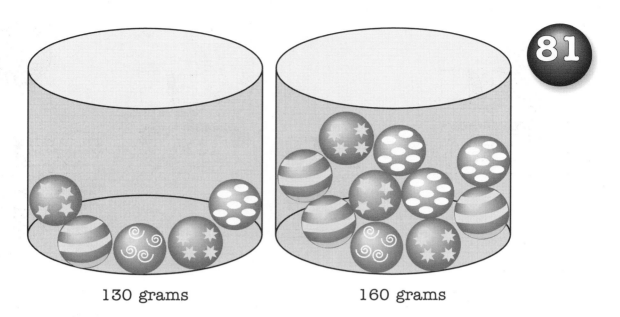

130 grams

160 grams

When they are empty, the cans weigh the same.

Each marble weighs the same amount.

How many grams is one marble?

- -

The birds are thinking of a pair of numbers.

What are the 2 numbers?

The least common multiple of the numbers is 36.

The greatest common factor is 6.

The sum is 30.

Three times my age is 2 less than 227.
My grandson is one fifth as many
years old as I am.
What is my grandson's age?

When you divide my number
by 5 and add 8, you get 72.

Pick a letter to stand for my number.

Write an equation to show this relationship.

What's my number?

Let *P* stand for the price of a box of granola.

You buy 3 boxes of granola and a box of crackers.

You pay with a $20 bill.

Write an equation to tell how much change, *C*, you will get.

Flight 27 took off with 1 empty seat for every 6 occupied seats.

There are 55 more occupied seats than empty seats.

How many of the seats are occupied?

Empty	1	2	3	4		
Occupied	6	12				
Difference	5	10				

There are twice as many women as men at the concert.

There are twice as many men as children at the concert.

Write a sentence that tells the number of children as compared to the number of women at the concert.

- -

There are numbers hidden under X, Y, and Z.

The numbers in the circles are sums of pairs of hidden numbers.

For example, the sum of X and Y is 31.

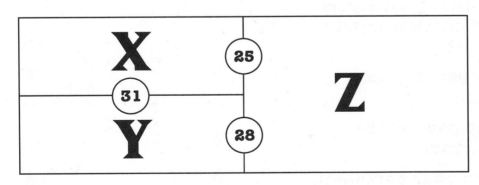

X = _____   Y = _____   Z = _____

How did you figure out the hidden numbers?

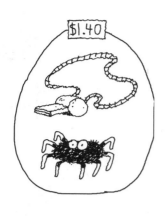

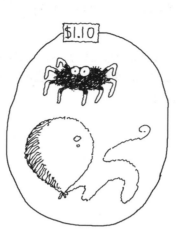

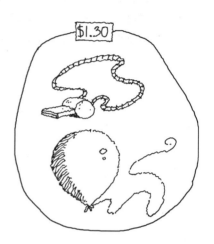

What is the price of the toy spider?

- -

Work with a partner.

Describe the arrow rule from the input set to the output set.

Now make up an arrow rule for another input-output set.

Show 5 pairings for your rule.

Give the pairings to your partner.

Describe your partner's rule.

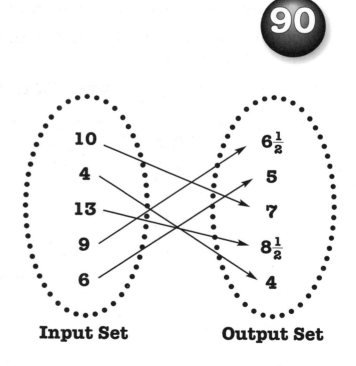

Input Set   **Output Set**

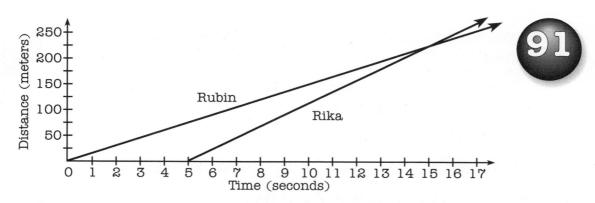

91

The graph shows the distance Rubin and Rika bicycled in the first seconds of the race.

- Who started first?

- How many meters had Rubin traveled when Rika started cycling?

- When Rika passed Rubin, how many meters were they from the starting line?

- Who do you think won the race?

- -

Add across. Add down.

The numbers in the circles are the row and column sums.

92

Angel and Angelique have birthdays on the same day.

- The sum of their ages is the greatest square number less than 40.

- Both of their ages are prime numbers.

- Angelique is 2 years older than Angel.

How old are Angel and Angelique?

93

94

What is the last digit of 8^1? 8^2? 8^3? 8^4? 8^5? 8^6? 8^7?

What will be the last digit of 8^{59}?

Tell how you decided.

Follow the flowchart.

- What is the end number when the start number is 29?

- What is the end number when the start number is 98?

- What is the start number when the end number is 3615?

How can you tell the start number when you know the end number?

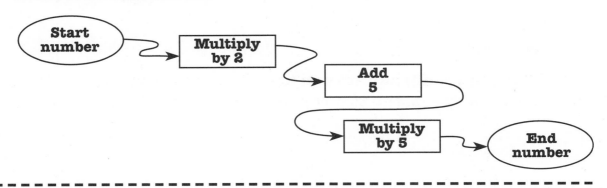

Start number → **Multiply by 2** → **Add 5** → **Multiply by 5** → **End number**

What is the length of a side of the square?

- The square has a perimeter of less than 50 inches.

- The area of the square is greater than 25 square inches.

- The length of a side is a whole number of inches.

Find all possible solutions.

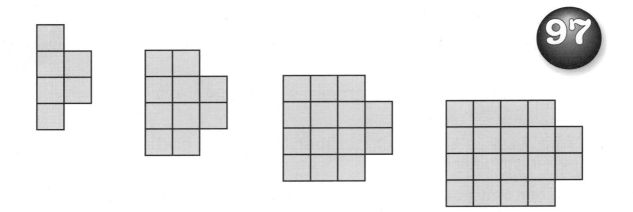

The pattern continues.

If there are 82 squares in the figure, how many squares are in the top row of that figure?

There is more than one unicycle, one bicycle, and one tricycle in the Cycle Shop window.

- How many tricycles are in the window?

- How many bicycles are in the window?

- How many unicycles are in the window?

Tell your thinking steps.

Each table shows the distance of a car from school after a given number of seconds.

99

Car 1

Seconds	Feet
1	22
2	52
3	92
4	138
5	188
6	240

Car 2

Seconds	Feet
1	4200
2	4240
3	4280
4	4320
5	4360
6	4400

Car 3

Seconds	Feet
1	350
2	320
3	290
4	260
5	230
6	200

Which car is traveling toward the school?

Which car is increasing its distance from the school at a steady rate?

- -

10% of 100 = ___% of 50

100

20% of 100 = ___% of 50

So, 50% of 100 = ___% of 50

and 100% of 100 = ___% of 50

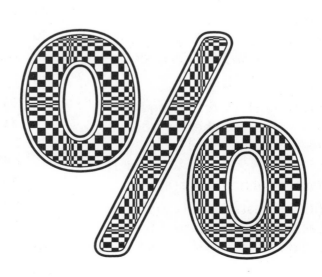

 # Answers

1. Jonas, Jared, Jeff, Jed, Jin Lee

2. 80; Explanations and questions will vary.

3. 3 × input − 1 = output; New rules will vary.

4. 46 sit-ups

5. No; since $A > B$ and $B > C$, A must be $> C$; and since $A > C$ and $C > D$, A must be $> D$.

6. There is an infinite number of answers; in each, 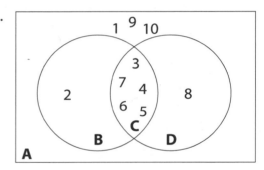 is twice the weight of △ and 3 times the weight of ▯.

7. July 15

8. 12 checks; Steps will vary.

9. 0, 8, 8 or 1, 7, 8 or 2, 6, 8 or 3, 5, 8 or 4, 4, 8

10. 21

11. 28

12. $1.60; Possible explanations:
    - Replace the 2 🔷 in the first chain with 1 ⬭. Then 3 ⬭ = $1.20, so 1 ⬭ = 40¢ and 1 🎲 = 20¢.
    - Replace each ⬭ in the first chain with 2 🔷. Then 6 🎲 = $1.20, so 1 🎲 = 20¢ and 1 ⬭ = 40¢.

13. 1 squiggle = 1 jiggle

14. Possible story: Jim is first riding at a constant speed. Then he slows down and rides at a slow speed for a while. Then he speeds up again until he's traveling at his original speed.

15. 61 seats, 960 seats; Possible explanation: Each row has a number of seats equal to double the row number, plus 1. The number of the last seat in row 30 is the number of seats in section A, and the last seat in each row has a number equal to (row number) × (row number + 2).

16. 300 vowels

17. 240

18. 9 guppies

19. 1, 6, 7

20. 11, 3; Explanations will vary; 14; $N − 8$

21. 4 inches

22.

```
            1  9  10
        ┌────────┐
        │     ┌──┼───┐
        │     │ 3│   │
        │   7 │ 4│ 8 │
        │ 2   │  │   │
        │   6 │ 5│   │
        │     │ C│   │
        │   B └──┼───┘D
        │A       │
        └────────┘
```

23. 25 squares; Explanations will vary.

24. | 4 ↗↗↗↗↗↗↗↖← = 81 |

    Note: Arrows can be in any order.

25. 18

26. 1b, 2c, 3a, 4d

27. 40¢

28. Possible pairs: 23, 45; 24, 44; 31, 37; 33, 35; Possible comparison: The difference between the lesser number and 34 is equal to the difference between the greater number and 34.

29. It doubles the first number and adds the second; 5, 17, 4, 4.

30. △ + 1, △ + 2, 133

31. If saving money is the reason for the choice, Ring-a-Ding; they would charge $5.60 while R.U. There? would charge $6.00.

32. 20

33. The end number is 10 times the start number.

    $2 \times \blacktriangle$

    $2 \times \blacktriangle + 10$

    $10 \times \blacktriangle + 50$

    $10 \times \blacktriangle$

34. 7 spiders, 4 ants

35. 12:00 noon

36. 6 grams, 3 grams; Explanations will vary.

37. 166; Explanations will vary.

38. Possible answer:

✦	2	4	6	8	10
✦	5	10	15	20	25

39. row 21; Possible explanation: The last seat in row 20 is numbered $20 \times 20 = 400$, and the last seat in row 21 is numbered $21 \times 21 = 441$, so seat 423 must be in row 21.

40. 150 in.^{2}

41. 6 mo

42. 206 white squares; Explanations will vary.

43. 151, m decreases, m increases

44. 560

45. 95

46. $750, $500

47. pyramid, sphere, cube; Possible explanation: In A, remove 2 🌐 and 1 ▲ from each side. Then ▲ is equal in weight to 2 🎲, so the ▲ weighs more than the 🎲. In B,

substitute 2 🎲 for the ▲. The 3 🌐 balance 4 🎲, so the 🌐 weighs more than the 🎲 but not as much as 2 🎲.

48. 1.7, 40.8, 14

49. $1.85, $3.10, $1.25, 60¢

50. Lists will vary; 23; Possible explanations: The sum of the seven numbers is 7 times the middle number. *Or,* the middle number is $\frac{1}{7}$ of the sum.

51. 149 letters

52. $6 \times$ input $- 1 =$ output

53. 800

54. 870 small white squares; Possible explanation: Square 28 has $30 \times 30 = 900$ small squares, of which 30 are black.

55. Possible answers: $- 10$, $\div 2$, or $\times \frac{1}{2}$; Explanations will vary.

56. Answers will vary, but the relationship must be a direct proportion. For example, it could show the relationship between the cost of a piece of wire and the length of the wire.

57.
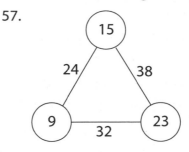

Explanations will vary.

58. $2; Explanations will vary.

59. 50¢, 60¢, 40¢; Explanations will vary.

60. from 7 through 21

61. 360 campers

62. 4 videos for $25; Possible explanations:
    - Compare unit costs: 3 for $20 is 1 for about $6.67; 4 for $25 is 1 for $6.25.
    - Find the cost of 12 videos (12 is the LCM of 3 and 4): 3 videos for

$20 is 12 for $80; 4 videos for $25 is 12 for $75.

63. 63 sports cards; Explanations will vary.

64. $304

65. 4, 16

66. $2.50

67. graph B

68. 5, 6, 8; Steps will vary.

69. row 10, column A; Explanations and questions will vary.

70. Pattern descriptions will vary; $(a \times c) = (b \times b) - 1$, or $(a \times c) + 1 = (b \times b)$.

71. $4.40, 3, 1, 12, 4, 20

72. $C = 40h + 50$, $350

73. It is multiplying the first number by 3 and adding the second number; 302, 90, 33.

74. 24

75. $52,800

76. 4

77. 390 or 480

78. 22; Explanations will vary.

79. from left to right: 3, 4, 8, 1

80. 302; Possible explanation: Multiply the building number by 6 and add 2.

81. 6 grams

82. 18 and 12

83. 15 years old

84. $n \div 5 + 8 = 72$; 320

85. Possible equation: $C = 20 - (3P + 1.29)$

86. 66 seats

87. Possible sentence: There are $\frac{1}{4}$ as many children as women.

88. 14, 17, 11; Explanations will vary.

89. 60¢

90. Each output equals $\frac{1}{2}$ the input plus 2. Rules will vary.

91. Rubin, 75 m, 225 m; If they continue at the same speeds, Rika won.

92. 9, 5, 6

93. 17 and 19 years old, respectively

94. 8, 4, 2, 6, 8, 4, 2; It will be a 2. Explanations will vary.

95. 315, 1005, 359; Explanations will vary.

96. 6, 7, 8, 9, 10, 11, or 12 in.

97. 20 squares

98. 7, 2, 2; Explanations will vary.

99. car 3, car 2

100. 20%, 40%, 100%, 200%